KS1 English Revision

Alison Head

Welcome to the magical world of Wizard Whimstaff – a wise wizard with great English powers!

Whimstaff wants to pass on his powers to you. He has some friends to help him.

Miss Snufflebeam – a forgetful young dragon who is always getting confused...

Pointy – Whimstaff's smart goblin assistant...

And Mugly and Bugly – Pointy's lazy pet frogs, who prefer eating and snoozing to learning, but still have a few tricks to teach you.

Just work your way through the pages of this book and you too will become a real English wizard like Wizard Whimstaff and his friends!

Good luck, young wizard!

Contents

Spelling, punctuation and grammar

Building vocabulary

⭐ Reading

⭐ Writing

Capital letters and full stops

Slurp! A **capital letter** shows where a **sentence** starts. A **full stop** shows where a sentence finishes.

Capital letters are special!

Croak! We use a capital letter at the start of a new sentence.

The magic spell was amazing.

It was dark when we got home.

Burp! We also use capital letters for the names of people, places, days of the week and months of the year.

The wand belongs to Wizard Whimstaff.

Have you see Miss Snufflebeam?

My birthday is in June.

I live in London.

Full stops end a sentence.

Is it time for a nap yet? We need a break! Full stops go at the end of sentences to show that they have finished.

> **Pointy tidies up.**

> **The cauldron was empty.**

Sometimes you use an **exclamation mark** instead of a full stop. This shows that something amazing or surprising is happening, or that someone is giving an order.

> **The spider was huge!**

> **Be quiet!**

If you are writing a question, you use a **question mark** at the end of the sentence, instead of a full stop.

> **Where is Pointy?**

Always start a new sentence with a capital letter.

MAGIC WORDS
capital letter · sentence
full stop · exclamation mark · question mark

Wizard's Practice

Workbook pages 4-5

Slurp! Underline the words in these sentences that should have capital letters. There may be more than one capital letter in each sentence.

1. are mugly and bugly hungry?
2. the magic hat was missing.
3. miss snufflebeam blew puffs of smoke.
4. wizard whimstaff cast a spell on monday.
5. pointy's birthday is in october.

Commas

Oh dear! I always get into a muddle with lists. **Commas** help to make lists easier to read.

⭐ Commas separate the items in a list.

If you need to include a list of things in a sentence, you should separate them with commas. The commas help people to read the items in the list more easily.

> **Dear Pointy,**
>
> **Please buy me an orange mouse food and wand polish.**
>
> **Love Wizard Whimstaff**

Oops! Without a comma, Pointy might try to buy an orange mouse! The list should read like this.

> **Dear Pointy,**
>
> **Please buy me an orange, mouse food and wand polish.**
>
> **Love Wizard Whimstaff**

There is no comma before the final **and**.

You should not use a comma before the final **and** in a list. That is because the **and** already separates the last two items, so you do not need a comma as well.

garlic

pepper

parsley

Pointy added garlic, pepper and parsley to the sauce.

Commas are also used to break sentences up, to make them easier to read.

MAGIC WORDS   comma

Wizard's Practice

Workbook pages 6-7

Can you help me by adding the commas to these sentences?

1. Mugly and Bugly love eating flies worms snails and bugs.

2. Wizard Whimstaff has a magic wand spell book and hat.

3. Pointy tidied up made dinner and ironed Wizard Whimstaff's cloak.

4. Mugly and Bugly are fat lazy greedy and rude!

5. Miss Snufflebeam collects pretty stones pressed flowers seashells and conkers.

Sentences

Slurp! Getting sentences just right is hard. If a sentence contains just one piece of information, it can be a bit boring. Use joining words to help join ideas together.

⭐ Joining words help to join ideas.

Burp! We often use joining words like **and** or **but** to join up pieces of information in our sentences. Different joining words do different jobs.

And joins two separate things that happen together.

> Wizard Whimstaff went out **and** Miss Snufflebeam followed.

But shows that although one thing happened, another thing did not.

> Pointy cast the spell **but** it did not work.

Other joining words show **when** things happened.

> Pointy tidied up **after** he had finished cooking tea.

Do not cram in too many ideas.

Putting too much information into a sentence will just make it untidy. It is best to stick to one or two main ideas, linked together with a joining word.

This sentence has four pieces of information in it. That is too many!

> Miss Snufflebeam was blowing puffs of smoke **and** filled up the cave with smoke **then** Pointy could not see where he was going **so** he fell over Mugly and Bugly.

It would be better to write it as two sentences instead.

> Miss Snufflebeam was blowing puffs of smoke **and** filled up the cave with smoke. Pointy could not see where he was going, **so** he fell over Mugly and Bugly.

If you think a sentence is getting too long, end it with a full stop and start a new one.

Wizard's Practice

Workbook pages 8–9

Croak! Underline the joining words in these sentences.

1. Mugly is fat, but Bugly is fatter.

2. Pointy mixed a potion and it bubbled noisily.

3. Wizard Whimstaff put on his magic cloak before he became invisible.

4. Miss Snufflebeam wears her diamond collar, because it is her favourite.

5. Pointy had a rest after he had finished all of his work.

Magic e

I love to do magic and so does the letter **e**! Hey presto!

⭐ **Magic e can change vowel sounds.**

Sometimes a magic **e** at the end of a word changes the sound made by the vowel in the middle of that word. A soft sound becomes a hard sound.

hop ➔ hope

mop ➔ mope

Can you hear the difference in the sound made by the **o**? Splendid!

Spotting that hard vowel sound in the middle of a word can give you a clue about how it is spelt. Remember, though, that other spelling patterns can make the same sound, so do not always assume you need a magic **e**!

tame   claim

 Vowels are the letters **a**, **e**, **i**, **o** and **u**. All the other letters of the alphabet are called consonants.

Magic **e** makes vowels say their name.

A useful way to think about what a magic **e** can do is to remember that the sound the middle vowel makes is the same as the **name** of the vowel.

A	snake
E	theme
I	mine
O	home
U	tune

MAGIC WORDS — vowel · consonant

Wizard's Practice

Workbook pages 10–11

Write down these magic **e** words.

1. ☆ _____

2. ☆ _____

3. ☆ _____

4. ☆ _____

5. ☆ _____

Verb endings **ed** and **ing**

Verbs are words that describe what is happening. They are action words. How they end tells us whether something is happening right now in the present, or if it happened in the past. Super!

⭐ You add **ing** to verbs to describe what is happening now.

Writing about things that are happening in the present is easy when you know how. Just add **ing** to the end of the verb!

go + **ing** = going

I am going to the park.

wait + **ing** = waiting

I am waiting for the teacher.

walk + **ing** = walking

I am walking to school.

⭐ You add **ed** to verbs to describe things that have already happened.

You will soon get the hang of writing about things that happened in the past. You can just add **ed** to the end of most verbs.

watch + **ed** = watched

I watched football yesterday.

paint + **ed** = painted

I painted a picture last week.

Some verbs do not end in **ed** when you are writing about the past. Find out about them later in the book.

MAGIC WORDS | verb

Wizard's Practice

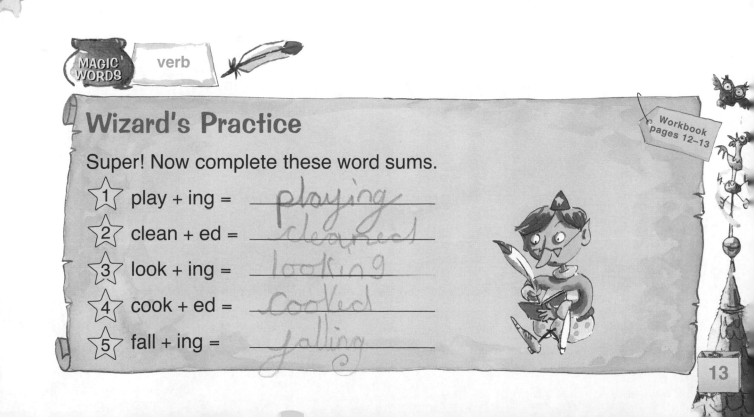

Workbook pages 12–13

Super! Now complete these word sums.

1. play + ing = _playing_
2. clean + ed = _cleaned_
3. look + ing = _looking_
4. cook + ed = _cooked_
5. fall + ing = _falling_

Plurals

Burp! **Plurals** are yummy. Two flies are better than one!

⭐ **Plural just means more than one of something.**

Croak! If you want to write about two or more of something, you need to use the plural form of the word.

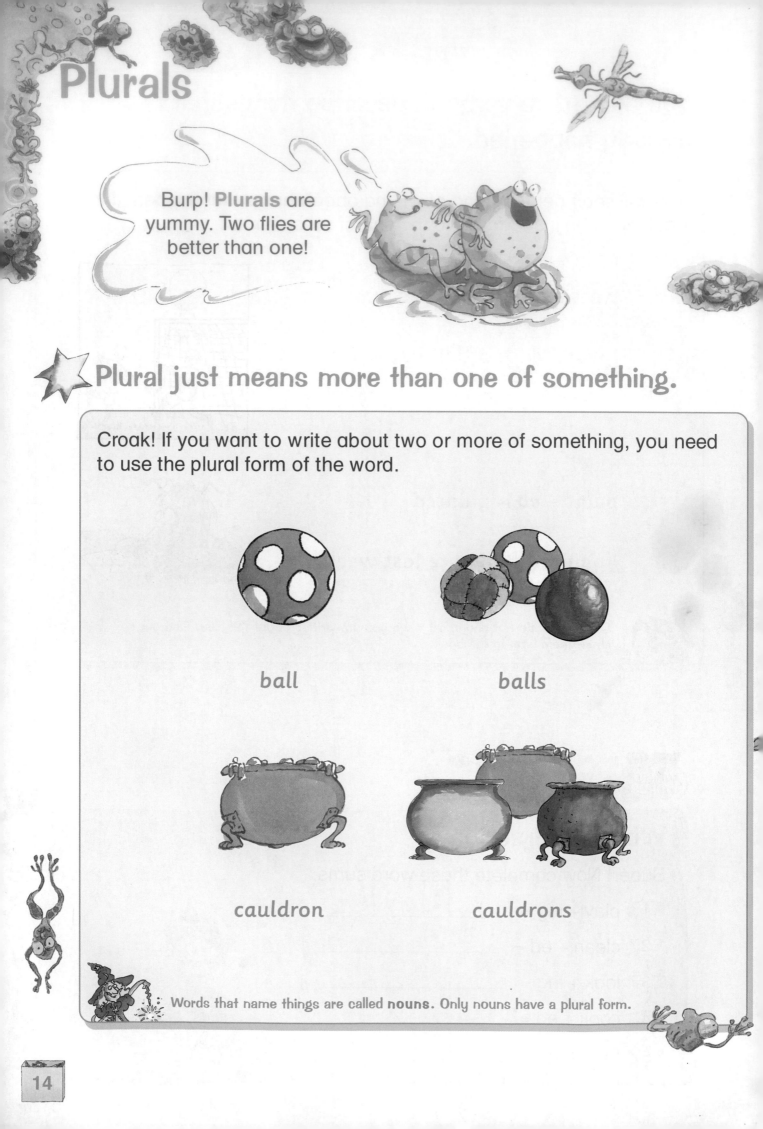

ball

balls

cauldron

cauldrons

Words that name things are called **nouns**. Only nouns have a plural form.

⭐ Most plurals end in s.

Slurp! To make something plural, you can usually just add an **s** to the end of the **singular** word.

wizard hat

wizard hats

pointed shoe

pointed shoes

Some plurals end in **es**, such as **dresses**. Watch out for these!

MAGIC WORDS plural · noun · singular

Wizard's Practice

Workbook pages 14–15

Write down the plurals of these words, while we have a snooze.

⭐ 1 _____

⭐ 2 _____

⭐ 3 _____

⭐ 4 _____

⭐ 5 _____

More about verb endings

You will find that some **past tense** verbs do not have the **ed** ending.

Some past tense verbs look like the present tense.

Spotting past tense verbs is easy when you know how! Lots end in **ed**, but some look almost the same as the **present tense** verb.

run	→	ran
fall	→	fell
swim	→	swam
hide	→	hid
sing	→	sung
hear	→	heard

If you have a problem spelling a past tense verb, try saying the word out loud to help you.

Other past tense verbs are totally different!

You will soon get the hang of spotting trickier past tense verbs. Some do not end in **ed**, or look anything like the present tense version. With these we just have to learn them.

go   ➡   went

see   ➡   saw

catch   ➡   caught

speak   ➡   spoke

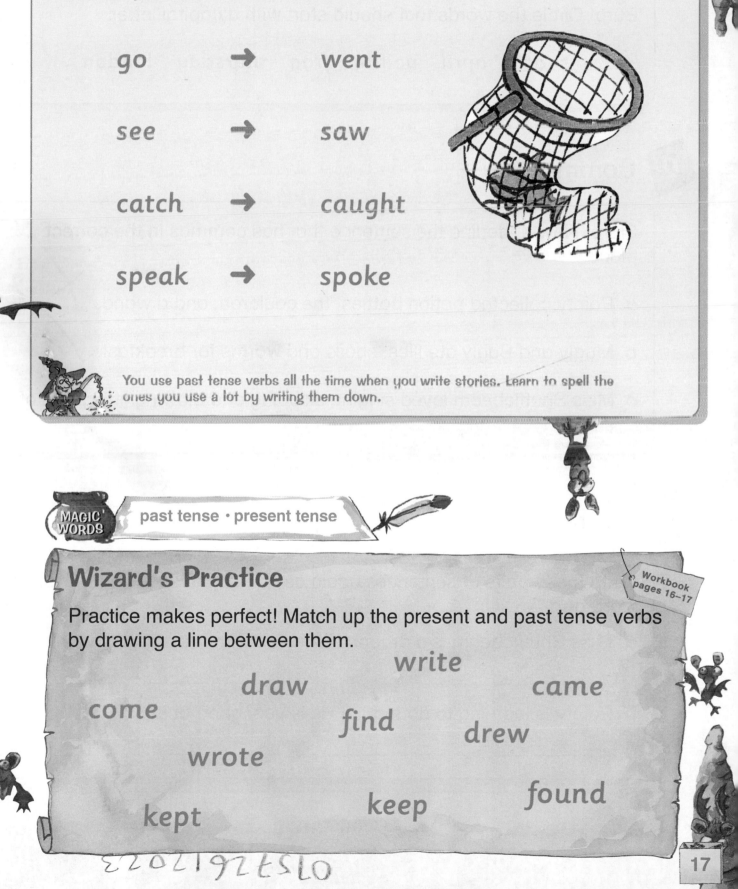

You use past tense verbs all the time when you write stories. Learn to spell the ones you use a lot by writing them down.

MAGIC WORDS | past tense · present tense

Wizard's Practice

Workbook
pages 16–17

Practice makes perfect! Match up the present and past tense verbs by drawing a line between them.

write

draw   came

come   find

                              drew

wrote

                    keep   found

kept

Wizard's Challenge

1 **Capital letters and full stops**

Burp! Circle the words that should start with a capital letter.

snack (april) pointy frog (thursday) (london)

2 **Commas**

Slurp! Now underline the sentence that has commas in the correct place.

a Pointy collected potion bottles, the cauldron, and a wand. ✓

b Mugly and Bugly ate flies, snails and worms for breakfast. ✓

c Miss Snufflebeam loved singing skipping and blowing little puffs of smoke.

3 **Sentences**

Write these pairs of sentences again as one sentence, using the joining word **and**.

a Miss Snufflebeam is a dragon. She lives with Wizard Whimstaff.

Miss snugglebeam is a dagon and she lives with wizun

b Pointy is learning to do magic. He is very good at it.

Pointy is learning to do mgic and he is very good.

4 Verb endings **ing** and **ed**

Add **ing** and **ed** to these verbs to complete the table, while we have a snack.

wash *washing* *washed*

jump *jumped* *jumping*

want *wanted* *wanting*

climb *climbing* *climbing*

5 Plurals

Circle the lily pads that contain plurals.

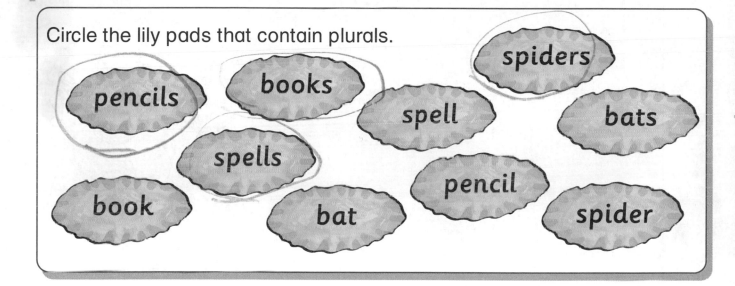

6 Past tense

Time for a nap! Can you underline the past tense verb in each pair for us?

a <u>took</u>   take   **d** drove   drive

b get   <u>got</u>   **e** <u>lost</u>   lose

c break   <u>broke</u>   **f** bring   <u>brought</u>

Synonyms

Let me tell you about **synonyms**, young wizard. They are words with similar meanings, like **fat** and **plump**.

Synonyms help you to describe things!

Lots of **adjectives**, or describing words, have synonyms that can help us to describe what things are like.

hot	→	warm
big	→	large
hungry	→	starving
small	→	tiny
fast	→	quick
nice	→	kind

Using synonyms saves you having to use the same describing words over and over again. It is a good idea to think of synonyms for adjectives you use a lot, like **big**, **small** and **nice** to stop your writing getting boring.

The little mouse held a little piece
of cheese in his little paws.

The little mouse held a small
piece of cheese in his tiny paws.

Verbs have synonyms too!

Allakazan! Let us look at verb synonyms. Verbs are doing or being words, like **run**, **swim** or **sleep**. They often have synonyms too, that can help you to describe exactly what someone or something is doing.

walk	→	stroll	pull	→	tug
sleep	→	doze	push	→	shove
run	→	jog		

Hey presto! Using synonyms stops you using the same verb too much.

While Miss Snufflebeam **ate** her snack, Mugly and Bugly **ate** theirs.

While Miss Snufflebeam **nibbled** her snack, Mugly and Bugly **gobbled** theirs.

Make a list of synonyms to use instead of words you use again and again.

MAGIC WORDS — synonym · adjective

Wizard's Practice

Workbook pages 18–19

Now have a go at writing down some wizard synonyms for these words.

1. cold _____
2. exhausted _____
3. beautiful _____
4. hurry _____
5. shout _____

Antonyms

We can use **antonyms** to describe the difference between things. Super!

Antonyms are just opposites.

Using antonyms is easy when you know how. They are just words with opposite meanings!

big   small   top   bottom

fast   slow   in   out

old   new

Antonyms can help us to describe things that are different.

Antonyms describe differences.

You will soon get the hang of using antonyms to describe the differences between things or people. If you put two antonyms together in a sentence, you can compare two things, or two people. You often use the joining word **but** in sentences like these.

This cauldron is full but this one is empty.

Wizard Whimstaff is tall
but Miss Snufflebeam is short.

You can find out how to use prefixes to make antonyms later in the book.

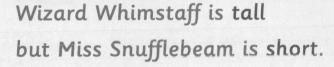

MAGIC WORDS | antonym

Wizard's Practice

Workbook pages 20–21

Practice makes perfect! Match up these pairs of antonyms with a line.

narrow

below   poor

heavy

on   light

rich

above   off

wide

Compound words

Oh dear! Have you noticed that some words look like two words stuck together?

Compound words are two words joined together.

Sometimes two words are joined together to make a new word. Wizard Whimstaff says that these are called **compound words**.

rain + bow = rainbow

hair + brush = hairbrush

neck + lace = necklace

Breaking up compound words can help you to spell them. Some really tricky words break up into smaller words that are easier to spell.

= cup + board   = door + knob

Try breaking new words up into compound words to see if it helps you to understand their meaning.

⭐ Think about what each word means.

Abracadada! Often, compound words take on a slightly different meaning than you might expect from the meaning of the separate words.

butterfly

handbag

armchair

Wizard's Practice

Workbook pages 22–23

Help! See if you can complete these word sums to make new compound words.

⭐1 pea + nut = _____

⭐2 tree + house = _____

⭐3 eye + lash = _____

⭐4 straw + berry = _____

⭐5 seat + belt = _____

Prefixes un and dis

Croak! **Prefixes** are groups of letters that go at the front of some words to change their meaning. **un** and **dis** are useful prefixes for making antonyms.

⭐ **un** and **dis** mean **not**.

Burp! The prefixes **un** and **dis** mean **not**. We add them to the start of some words to make antonyms, or opposite words.

un + happy = unhappy   unhappy means not happy

un + usual = unusual   unusual means not usual

dis + agree = disagree   disagree means not agree

dis + obey = disobey   disobey means not obey

dis + loyal = disloyal   disloyal means not loyal

Prefixes make spelling easy, because you can always add them to the start of the **root word** without having to change its spelling first.

You have to use the right prefix.

Now listen up! You cannot add **un** or **dis** to any word you like, or you will make words that make no sense at all!

unpink ✗

distall ✗

Even with words that you can add prefixes to, you still have to match the right prefix to the right word. Sounds like a job for Pointy!

✗ ✔ ✗ ✔

distidy untidy unhonest dishonest

When you are reading, see if you can spot other prefixes that can also make antonyms, e.g. incredible, impolite, anticlockwise.

MAGIC WORDS prefix · root word

Wizard's Practice

Workbook pages 24–25

We will have to call you Pointy soon! Choose **un** or **dis** to add to each of these words.

☆1 ____ appear

☆2 ____ kind

☆3 ____ sure

☆4 ____ popular

☆5 ____ qualify

Suffixes ly and ful

Suffixes are groups of letters that we can add to the end of some words to change their meaning. **ly** and **ful** are useful suffixes. Super!

There are spelling rules for adding ly and ful.

You will soon get the hang of adding **ly** and **ful** to words to change their meaning. Usually you can just add them to the end of the root word.

quick + ly = quickly

hope + ful = hopeful

sad + ly = sadly

play + ful = playful

If the root word ends in a consonant followed by **y**, you have to change the **y** to **i** first.

pretty + ly = prettily

beauty + ful = beautiful

happy + ly = happily

duty + ful = dutiful

Match the right suffix to the right word!

You have to match the right suffix to each word, or the new word you make will not make any sense. Practice makes perfect!

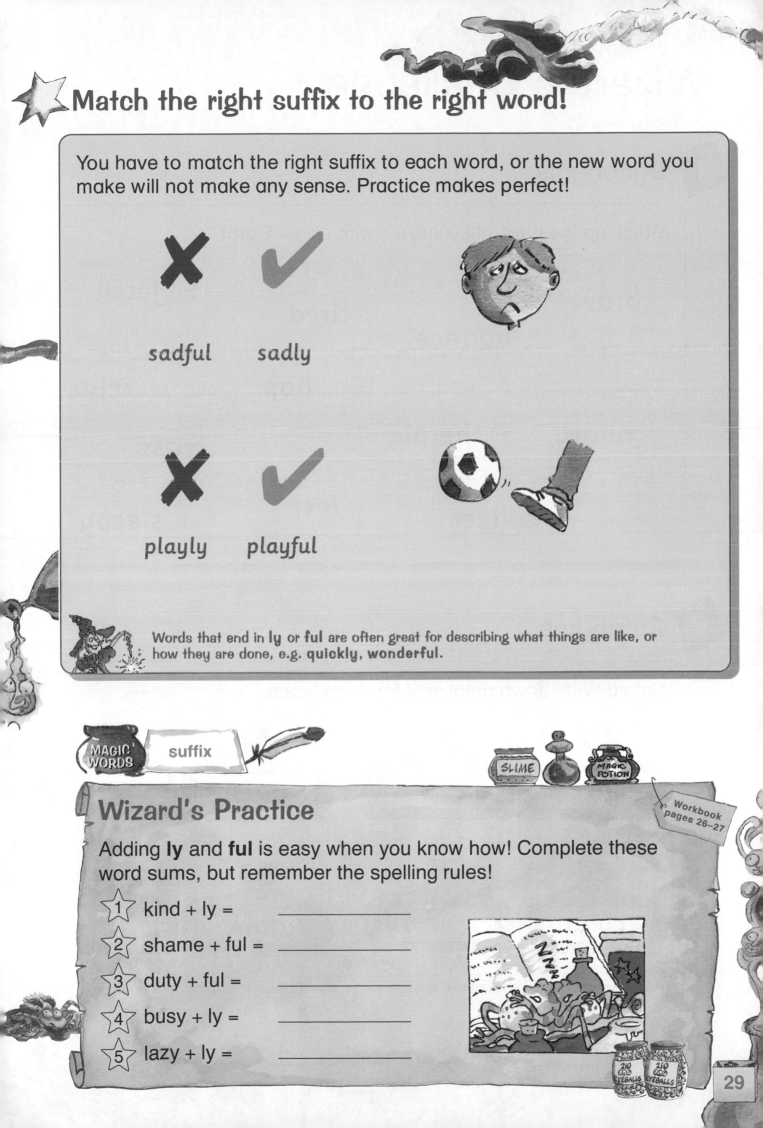

X sadful ✔ sadly

X playly ✔ playful

Words that end in **ly** or **ful** are often great for describing what things are like, or how they are done, e.g. **quickly**, **wonderful**.

MAGIC WORDS | suffix

Wizard's Practice

Workbook pages 26–27

Adding **ly** and **ful** is easy when you know how! Complete these word sums, but remember the spelling rules!

1 kind + ly = _____

2 shame + ful = _____

3 duty + ful = _____

4 busy + ly = _____

5 lazy + ly = _____

Wizard's Challenge

1 Synonyms

Match up the pairs of synonyms with a line. Slurp!

brave

bounce

tired

fetch

hop

relax

angry

heroic

cross

collect

rest

sleepy

2 Antonyms

Croak! Write down antonyms for these words.

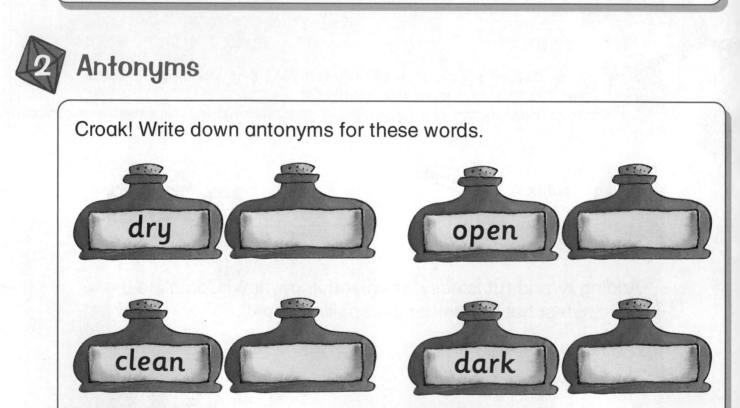

dry

open

clean

dark

3 Compound words

Is it time for a nap yet? Write down the words that make up each of these compound words, while we have a snooze.

a motorway   = _____ + _____

b footpath   = _____ + _____

c keyhole   = _____ + _____

4 Prefixes **un** and **dis**

Complete these words sums

a dis + approve = _____

b _____ + wise = unwise

c dis + like = _____

d _____ + well = unwell

e _____ + ability = disability

f un + do = _____

5 Suffixes **ly** and **ful**

Burp! Grub's up! Circle the plates that contain real words.

boldful

peaceful

joyly

colourly

restful

slowly

Reading tests

I find reading tests a bit scary! Do you?

Start by reading the texts.

In a reading test you will be given pieces of writing to read. Then there will be some questions to answer.

Some of them will be stories, or **fiction**, and some will be information, or **non-fiction**. There may be a poem as well.

You need to start by reading all of the pieces of writing really carefully. If you are reading a story, look out for things like the names of characters and where the story takes place.

If you are reading information, look for names and dates, and think about what the piece of writing is about. Underline key information on the paper, so that you can find it again easily when you answer the questions.

Our neighbours moved in at the beginning of <u>December</u>. Two huge lorries pulled up outside number 23, and men unloaded box after box of things and took them inside.

Some of the <u>boxes were a very strange shape</u> and I longed to know what was inside.

They were <u>two children</u> in the family and they came over the day after their moved in, to say hello. Their names were <u>Harry</u> and <u>Sam</u>.

Then read the questions.

Abracadada! You need to read all the questions carefully. Make sure you know what the question is asking before you try and answer it. Look for words in the questions that give you clues about the kind of information you need to find.

How?	Probably information about the way something was done.
What?	Maybe the name of something.
Where?	Look for the name of a place.
Who?	Probably the name of a person.
When?	Look for a day, date or time.

Read the whole question through carefully, so that you know exactly what you are looking for. Otherwise you will get confused!

 If you find it hard to read stories, information or poems, practise reading before a test.

MAGIC WORDS   fiction · non-fiction

Wizard's Practice

Workbook pages 28–29

Can you help me by matching up these questions with a possible answer by drawing a line between them?

1. How do moles dig tunnels?   During the rainy summer months.

2. What is a mole hill?   With their powerful paws.

3. Where do moles live?   Professor Diggs.

4. Who is a mole expert?   A pile of earth dug out to make a tunnel.

5. When are you most likely to see a mole?   Under the ground in tunnels.

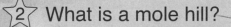

Answering test questions

Answering the questions in a reading test is easy when you know how!

There are different types of questions.

You will soon get the hang of answering the different types of questions on a reading test paper. Some questions ask you to choose the best answer from a choice of three or four. Often you just have to tick a box, rather than writing anything down.

Some questions ask you to find and copy a word, or say why a word has been used. You need to look at the whole sentence to answer this type of question.

Sometimes you just have to write down a word or two for an answer. Other times you might need to write a sentence. The question will tell you what you need to do, so read it carefully.

1 **Do you think Miss Snufflebeam was afraid?**

   Write yes or no.

   Yes.

2 **Why do you think Pointy called the police?**

   Because he could not find a way into the house to rescue Miss Snufflebeam.

You do not need to guess the answers!

Remember, the answer to the question will always be there if you look hard enough. So if you cannot spot the answer, take a deep breath and read through the writing again slowly. Practice makes perfect!

See if the wording of the question can help you to find the information you need.

> The return of swallows and swifts is a sign that spring is here.

Often the questions mirror the words in the piece of writing.

> What does the writer say is a sign that spring is here?

Remember to always write neatly, so people can read your answers!

Wizard's Practice

Workbook pages 30–31

Super! Read these sentences about answering questions on a reading test paper, and write **True** or **False** after each one.

1. Neat handwriting is important. _____

2. There is only one type of question on a reading test paper. _____

3. Sometimes you just need to pick the best answer from a selection. _____

4. The answer is always in the text somewhere. _____

5. You will always have to write a lot for each answer. _____

35

Tackling new words

Do you know what
to do if there
is a word you do
not know in a test?

⭐ **Learning new words is fun!**

Abracadada! Use the other information in the text to help you to work out a new word.

Look at this sentence. I do not know what the word **predators** means. Do you?

Hedgehogs have prickles

to protect them from

predators like foxes.

I know that prickles are sharp and the writing says that they protect the hedgehog, so the fox must want to hurt it. Perhaps the fox wants to eat the hedgehog? Yuk! I think a predator might be an animal that eats another one.

I can use the picture to help me too. The fox looks scary!

 If you need to use a new word in an answer, copy it carefully, so that you spell it correctly.

Test your idea.

The word predators appears again in this piece of writing, so I can test my idea with that sentence too.

Barn owls are very clever night-time predators, using their excellent night vision to track their prey. They eat mice and voles.

So, owls are **predators**, because they eat mice and voles. There is another new word there too. **Prey** must be the animals that a **predator** eats. Abracadada!

Workbook pages 32–33

Wizard's Practice

Put a tick by each statement that can help you to work out a new word.

1. Just guess. ☐

2. Look at the rest of the sentence. ☐

3. Use the picture. ☐

4. Assume that it means **handbag**. ☐

5. Test your ideas with other sentences. ☐

Wizard's Challenge

1 Reading tests

Slurp! Write **fiction** or **non-fiction** after each of these sentences, to say what kind of writing you think it comes from.

a Ben picked up the magic box and hid it in his school bag.   _____

b Tortoises hibernate during the winter.   _____

c Henry VIII had six wives.   _____

d Molly watched the countryside fly past, out of the train window.   _____

e Chris and Tom realised that they were locked in the ghostly museum!   _____

f Eating fruit and vegetables is very good for you.   _____

2 Tackling new words

Looking at unfamiliar words in their sentences can help you to work out what they mean. You probably know these words, but can you fit them into the right sentence?

> parachute   badminton   organic   relatives   spaghetti

a We had _____ with tomato sauce for tea.

b Mum and Dad are playing _____ tonight.

c All of my _____ are coming for Gran's birthday.

d Our teacher did a _____ jump at the weekend.

e Mum always buys _____ food.

Answering test questions

Burp! See if you can find the answers to these questions in the piece of text.

Green fingers

Lots of people enjoy growing their own fruit and vegetables because they think it tastes better. Growing your own food is good exercise as well, as there is always a lot of digging to do.

Many people rent allotments from their local council to give them more space to grow food. Allotments are patches of land that you can rent to grow food on. It takes a lot of hard work to keep an allotment, because they are much larger than most gardens.

a Why do lots of people enjoy growing their own fruit and vegetables?

_____

b Why is growing your own food good exercise?

_____

c Why do many people rent allotments from their local council?

_____

d What is an allotment?

_____

e Why does it take a lot of hard work to keep an allotment?

_____

Characters

Characters are the people in a story, so writing about them is important.

⭐ Characters make a story happen.

The people in stories are called characters. What they say and do makes the story happen. They should also make it exciting to read!

If you can make your characters seem real, your readers will want to find out what happens to them. You need to think about how they would behave if they were real people, so that you make what they do seem believable. Super!

Miss Snufflebeam gobbled a huge plate of dinner, then burped loudly. Mugly and Bugly, who were playing nicely nearby, looked shocked.

That does not sound right at all! These sentences do not fit with what we know about Miss Snufflebeam or Mugly and Bugly, so it is hard for us to imagine that they are true.

⭐ Describe your characters carefully.

Describing characters is easy when you know how! You need to think about how they feel, as well as what they say and do.

Describing words can help your reader to imagine your characters more clearly.

Wizard Whimstaff flicked through his spell book.

This is okay, but it does not really tell us very much about Wizard Whimstaff. Look what happens if we add some describing words.

*Clever Wizard Whimstaff flicked through his **magic** spell book excitedly.*

 If you ever have a problem making up characters, think about people you know and base the characters on them.

Wizard's Practice

Workbook pages 34–35

Match up the characters with actions that you think are believable. Use what you already know about them, to help you to decide.

1	Mugly	tidied up carefully.
2	Miss Snufflebeam	gobbled up Bugly's snack.
3	Wizard Whimstaff	croaked at Mugly.
4	Bugly	cast a wonderful spell.
5	Pointy	skipped happily off to play.

Speech

Making your characters talk to each other is a brilliant way of bringing them to life. Hey presto!

⭐ Use speech marks for speech.

Real people speak to each other all the time, so the characters in our stories need to talk too, or they will not seem very real.

When you write the words that a character says, you have to use **speech marks**. They go right round what the character says.

"We are hungry," complained Mugly and Bugly.

"My head hurts," sighed Miss Snufflebeam.

Speech marks are important, because they tell your reader that someone is speaking.

 Speech marks always go in pairs, at the beginning **and** the end of what your character says.

42

Do not always use the word **said**!

Listen carefully, young wizard. Using the word **said** all the time is very boring. You need to think about how your characters talk, as well as what they say, to help you to think of better words. For example, are they whispering or are they shouting?

"Where is my wand?" asked Pointy.

"I saw it yesterday," replied Miss Snufflebeam.

Swapping **said** for a better word will work like magic to make your writing exciting.

Make a list of words to use in your stories instead of **said**.

MAGIC WORDS | speech marks

Workbook pages 36–37

Wizard's Practice

Now let us see if you can pick a good word from the cauldron to complete each sentence.

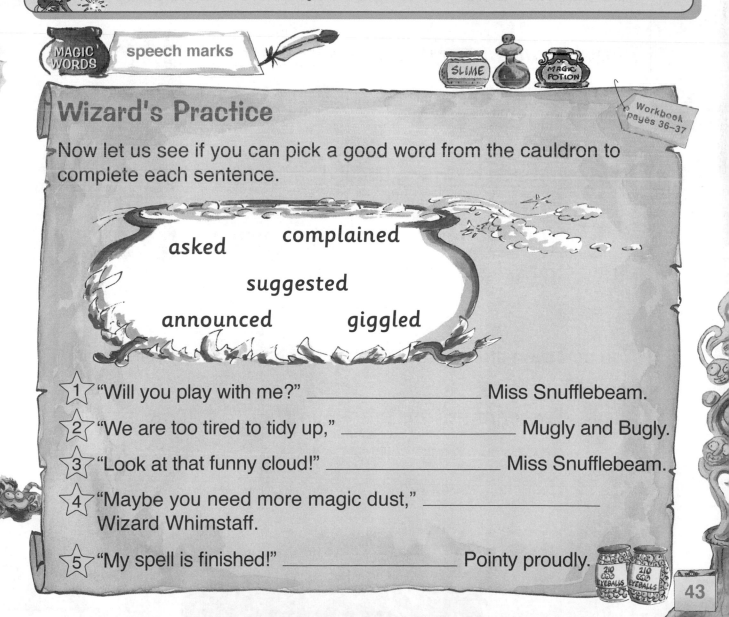

asked   complained

suggested

announced   giggled

1 "Will you play with me?" _____ Miss Snufflebeam.

2 "We are too tired to tidy up," _____ Mugly and Bugly.

3 "Look at that funny cloud!" _____ Miss Snufflebeam.

4 "Maybe you need more magic dust," _____ Wizard Whimstaff.

5 "My spell is finished!" _____ Pointy proudly.

43

Starting and finishing stories

Starting and finishing a story properly is really important, but how do I do it?

How to begin your story.

The start of a story should be really exciting, so your readers want to find out what happens next.

You can start a story by talking about where it takes place.

Twin Gables Hotel stood right by a beautiful beach.

Or you can start by writing about a character.

Sam had always wanted to play in the school football team.

You can even start by talking about when the story happened.

We were having tea when the doorbell rang. "I wonder who that is," said Mum.

Plan your story before you start, so that you know how it will start and finish, and what will happen in the middle.

Keep going right to the end!

Writing a good story ending can be tricky. You cannot just stop writing. You have to make sure that something happens to end the story properly, so that your reader will know when it has finished.

Your ending needs to follow on from the rest of the story, so that it is believable. Often, your main characters will have learnt something in their adventure and this is where you tell your reader what that is.

Beginning	Katy is playing with her dog in the house.
Middle	Katy throws a ball for the dog and it breaks a vase.
Ending	Katy tells her mum what happened, and promises not to play with a ball in the house again.

Wizard's Practice

Workbook pages 38~39

Can you help me to tick the sentences that are true?

1. You can start a story by writing about a character. ☐

2. The start of a story is not important. ☐

3. You should plan how you will start and finish, before you start to write. ☐

4. It does not matter if your reader does not realise that the story has finished. ☐

5. The ending has to follow on from the rest of the story. ☐

Information writing

Burp! Writing that is not a story is often meant to share information with people.

⭐ **Information is facts.**

Croak! Information writing is based on facts, rather than on what you think. Newspapers often contain facts.

When you write information, you need to collect facts and organise them so that they make sense for your reader. Slurp!

You need to start with a title which says what the writing is about. Then you need an introduction that explains a bit more about it.

Rare Wildlife

This report is about how many British birds and animals are becoming very rare because of the way we care for the environment.

The end of a piece of information is the one place where you can sometimes say what you think.

Changes to the way land is farmed are helping to save some of our rarest animals. I am glad that people are trying to help them.

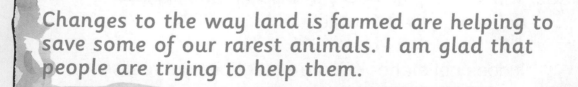

You need to organise the information!

Slurp! You should not just fill a piece of information writing with facts. You need to organise them, to make them easier for your reader to understand. That sounds like a job for Pointy!

Sub-headings break up the information.
Bullet points help you to list pieces of information.

Elephants

General information ←

- Elephants are the largest land animal.
- They live in Africa and Asia.

Elephant facts ←

- Elephants can weigh as much as a bus.
- They can suck up more than 11 litres of water with their trunk.
- They eat grass, small branches and the bark from trees.

Elephants use their long trunks to suck up water.

Information texts often include pictures. They need special labels called captions which explain the picture.

Wizard's Practice

Workbook pages 40–41

Circle the things you might find in information writing.

1. lots about how the writer feels
2. a title
3. bullet points
4. made-up characters
5. sub-headings

Instructions

There are lots of different types of instructions and they are all great for telling people how to do things. Allakazan!

⭐ Order is everything!

Listen carefully, young wizard. When you are writing instructions, you have to break down the task into several steps.

It is important that you describe the steps in the right order, or your readers will get into a muddle!

How to mix a potion

1 Pour the ingredients out carefully.

2 Find a clean potion bottle.

3 Mix the ingredients together.

If Pointy had followed these instructions, he would have poured the ingredients out all over the table before he had a bottle to put them in!

Numbering the steps makes it really clear which order they come in.

Instructions must be written clearly!

Hey presto! When you write instructions, make sure you describe what your reader has to do very carefully.

Instructions should have a title, so that your reader knows what they are going to do.

You need to be accurate too. Words like **about halfway up**, or **after a few minutes** are not very helpful! Look at the specific information in these instructions.

To make a vanishing spell

Add half a tub of crushed snail shell
to one bottle of magic spring water.

Boil in a cauldron for 30 minutes.

Allow to cool for 3 hours.

Wizard's Practice

Workbook pages 42–43

Number these instructions for feeding Mugly and Bugly 1-5.

1 ____ Put equal portions of worm slop into the bowls.

2 ____ Stand back while they eat, so that you do not get splashed.

3 ____ Put the bowls down, making sure that you give each frog the right bowl.

4 ____ Wash the bowls, floor and walls when they have finished.

5 ____ Find their favourite food bowls.

Letters

I know that letters are written messages you send to people, but how do you write them?

⭐ Set your letters out properly!

Apparently there is a special way to set out letters. Look at this letter from Pointy.

Put your address here ➡

**Apprentice Academy
High Mountain
HM12 CC1**

Put the date here ➡ **12th June**

Dear Miss Snufflebeam, ⬅ Put who the letter is to here

I am having a lovely time at the apprentice wizard summer school. This morning we learnt how to turn a frog into a prince, so I will try that spell on Mugly and Bugly when I get back!

Lots of love,

Pointy ⬅ Write your name here

Think who the letter is for.

When you write a letter, you have to match the sort of words you use to the person you are writing to.

If you are writing to a friend, you can use friendly language.

> Hi!
>
> How are you?
>
> See you soon.
>
> Lots of love,

If you are writing to somebody you do not know, you have to use more formal language.

> I hope that you can help.
>
> It was very nice to meet you.
>
> Kind regards,

There are not as many rules for writing emails and text messages.

Wizard's Practice

Workbook pages 44–45

Oops! Do you think you can find these things in my letter to Pointy? Underline these features on the letter when you find them.

1. The date.
2. Who the letter is to.
3. Who the letter is from.
4. The address of the person writing the letter.
5. What the letter is saying thank you for.

Dark Cave
Precipice
Spelltown
SP11 0FP

15th June

Dear Pointy,

Thanks for your letter. I would love to live with two handsome princes instead of Mugly and Bugly!

See you soon,

Miss Snufflebeam

Wizard's Challenge

1 Characters

Burp! Choose a verb from the brackets to describe what these characters might do. Underline the verb you choose. Think carefully about each character before you choose.

a The old lady (*skipped / hobbled*) across the road.

b The teacher (*scribbled / wrote*) neatly on the board.

c The shopkeeper (*tidied / messed*) up the shelves.

2 Speech

This looks like a job for Pointy! Add the speech marks to these sentences.

a Well done! congratulated Wizard Whimstaff.

b Where is Pointy? asked Miss Snufflebeam.

c Look at this pretty flower! exclaimed Miss Snufflebeam.

3 Starting and finishing stories

Croak! See if you can work out whether these sentences come from the start or the finish of a story. Write **S** or **F** in the box at the end of each one.

a It was morning when the snow began to fall.

b The door slammed shut and the wicked queen was trapped inside forever.

c We climbed aboard the lifeboat and headed back to the shore, safe at last.

4 Information writing

Slurp! These are all features you might find in a piece of information writing. Draw lines to match each one with the job that it does.

a bullet points   says what the piece of writing is about

b title   help you to list facts clearly

c sub-heading   your chance to give your view

d introduction   breaks the topic up into smaller sections

e ending   says more about what the piece of writing is about

5 Instructions

Listen up! Instructions need specific information to make them clear. Underline the specific bits of information in these instructions.

a Heat 1 litre of water.

b Add 100g of sugar and the juice of three lemons.

c Simmer for five minutes.

6 Letters

Is it time for a nap yet? Look at these sentences about letters and underline the ones you think are true.

a You put your address on letters you write.

b You put the date on.

c You use the same kinds of words whoever the letter is to.

d Emails have to be set out just like a letter.

Test Practice

There are some words missing from this piece of text about a trip to the zoo. Ask a helper to read the finished version from the answers section for you and then fill in the missing words.

Daisy was excited because she was _____ to the zoo. As she queued _____ with Mum she could hear monkeys chattering inside, and over the top of the _____ she could see an elephant's trunk _____ in the air.

Inside, the _____ was full of people looking at all the animals. Daisy watched the penguins _____ fed. She turned to speak to Mum, but Mum was not there!

Daisy looked and _____ but she could not _____ Mum. Then she saw something strange. A monkey in a _____ was waving at her and pointing at something. Daisy looked again and _____ that the monkey was pointing at Mum!

54

Building vocabulary

Read the piece of writing and answer the questions.

Zoe stepped into the dark cave, leaving the bright sunshine behind.

Spotlights lit up beautiful shapes in the stone and the tour guide explained that some people think that an ugly witch was turned to stone in the cave, long ago.

The air felt cool and damp as they went further into the cave and Zoe was chilly. She wished she had brought a cosy jumper.

1 Find and copy a word which has an opposite meaning to **dark**.

_____

2 Find and copy a word which has an opposite meaning to **beautiful**.

_____

3 Find and copy two words which describe how cold it is in the cave.

_____   _____

4 Think of another word the writer could have used to describe Zoe's jumper.

_____

★ Reading

Read this piece of text, then answer the questions.

"Saturday! Fantastic!" Kirstie looked forward to Saturday all week. All she had ever wanted to be was a ballerina, and every Saturday she would gobble her breakfast and pull on her pink leotard and tights, ready for her class.

Kirstie went to ballet with her friend Meghan, who lived across the road. Kirstie liked Meghan, but secretly thought that she was not a very good dancer. She would fling her legs about and throw her arms this way and that. Sometimes Kirstie thought that she looked more like a frog than a dancer!

The girls walked together to their class, and today it was raining. "Let's take a short cut down Squire Street," suggested Kirstie. The girls ran along, trying to keep dry. Suddenly, a large van sped past, right through a huge puddle at the edge of the road. Muddy water sprayed up all over Kirstie's ballet clothes.

"Oh no!" she cried. "Look at me, I'm filthy!" "Never mind that," said Meghan, pulling at Kirstie's arm. "We have to get to ballet. Mrs Simms is giving us our parts in the show today."

Kirstie stumbled unhappily to ballet. She looked a mess, and she was cold. Still, she was sure to get the lead part in the show, and then she would feel better. Imagine if she was chosen to play Cinderella! Lost in her daydream, Kirstie forgot the drizzle.

1 What day did Kirstie do ballet?

_____

2 Why did she gobble her breakfast?

_____

3 fling and **throw**

What do these words tell us about Meghan's dancing?
Underline your answer.

that she throws things while she dances

that she is not very elegant

that she is doing a special dance

that she is better at dancing than Kirstie

4 Why does Kirstie think that Meghan looks like a frog when she dances? Underline your answer.

because she has green skin

because she hops a lot

because the way she moves her arms and legs looks like a frog

because Kirstie does not like her

5 Who said these things? Draw a line to Kirstie or Meghan.

"Saturday! Fantastic!"

"Look at me, I'm filthy!"

Meghan

"Never mind that."

Kirstie

"We have to get to ballet."

6 Where do the girls go to take their short cut?

_____

_____

7 What is the name of the girls' ballet teacher?

_____

8 Find and copy two words that describe the weather.

_____   _____

9 Why did Kirstie forget the rain?

_____

_____

10 What part does Kirstie hope to play in the show?

_____

_____

**1 Look at this story outline. How do you think the story will end?
Write your idea for an ending in the box.**

Beginning

Daniel's neighbour has a new puppy. He asks if he can take it for a walk. He takes it to the park.

Middle

At the park, the puppy sees another dog and runs away. Daniel chases after it, but he cannot find it. He has to go and tell his neighbour.

Ending

Helpful notes

2 Now have a go at writing the story.

3 Now imagine that you are Daniel. Write a letter to a friend, telling them about what happened. Remember the rules for setting out letters!

Answers

Page 5

1 Are Mugly and Bugly hungry?

2 The magic hat was missing.

3 Miss Snufflebeam blew puffs of smoke.

4 Wizard Whimstaff cast a spell on Monday.

5 Pointy's birthday is in October.

Page 7

1 Mugly and Bugly love eating flies, worms, snails and bugs.

2 Wizard Whimstaff has a magic wand, spell book and hat.

3 Pointy tidied up, made dinner and ironed Wizard Whimstaff's cloak.

4 Mugly and Bugly are fat, lazy, greedy and rude!

5 Miss Snufflebeam collects pretty stones, pressed flowers, seashells and conkers.

Page 9

1 Mugly is fat, <u>but</u> Bugly is fatter.

2 Pointy mixed a potion <u>and</u> it bubbled noisily.

3 Wizard Whimstaff put on his magic cloak <u>before</u> he became invisible.

4 Miss Snufflebeam wears her diamond collar, <u>because</u> it is her favourite.

5 Pointy had a rest <u>after</u> he had finished all of his work.

Page 11

1 gate   4 knife

2 rope   5 mice

3 bone

Page 13

1 playing   4 cooked

2 cleaned   5 falling

3 looking

Page 15

1 cats   4 dragons

2 bottles   5 frogs

3 wands

Page 17

come → came

draw → drew

find → found

write → wrote

keep → kept

Pages 18–19

Wizard's Challenge

1 Circled words should be:

April, Pointy, Thursday, London

2 The underlined sentence should be **b**.

3 **a** Miss Snufflebeam is a dragon and she lives with Wizard Whimstaff.

  b Pointy is learning to do magic and he is very good at it.

4 **wash**   washing   washed

  jump   jumping   jumped

  want   wanting   wanted

  climb   climbing   climbed

5 The circled lily pads should be:

pencils   bats

spiders   spells

books

6 **a** took   **d** drove

  b got   **e** lost

  c broke   **f** brought

Page 21

Answers may vary, but examples are:

1 freezing   4 rush

2 tired   5 yell

3 pretty

Page 23

heavy → light

rich → poor

on → off

wide → narrow

above → below

Page 25

1 peanut   4 strawberry

2 treehouse   5 seatbelt

3 eyelash

Page 27

1 disappear   4 unpopular

2 unkind   5 disqualify

3 unsure

Page 29

1 kindly   4 busily

2 shameful   5 lazily

3 dutiful

Pages 30–31

Wizard's Challenge

1 brave → heroic

  tired → sleepy

  angry → cross

  hop → bounce

  collect → fetch

  rest → relax

2 Answers may vary, but examples are:

  dry → wet

  clean → dirty

  open → shut

  dark → light

3 **a** motor + way

  b foot + path

  c key + hole

4 **a** disapprove   **d** unwell

  b unwise   **e** disability

  c dislike   **f** undo

5 Circled words should be **peaceful**, **restful** and **slowly**.

Page 33

1 How do moles dig tunnels?
With their powerful paws.

2 What is a mole hill?
A pile of earth dug out to make a tunnel.

3 Where do moles live?
Under the ground in tunnels.

4 Who is a mole expert?
Professor Diggs.

5 When are you most likely to see a mole?
During the rainy summer months.

Pag 35

1 True

2 False

3 True

4 True

5 False

Page 37

Ticked statements should be:

2 Look at the rest of the sentence.

3 Use the picture.

5 Test your ideas with other sentences.

Pages 38–39

Wizard's Challenge

1 Fiction: a, d, e
  Non-fiction: b, c, f

2 **a** spaghetti
  b badminton
  c relatives
  d parachute
  e organic

3 **a** because they think it tastes better
  b because there is lots of digging to do
  c because it gives them more space to grow food
  d a patch of land you rent to grow food on
  e because they are much larger than most gardens

Page 41

1 Mugly gobbled up Bugly's snack.

2 Miss Snufflebeam skipped happily off to play.

3 Wizard Whimstaff cast a wonderful spell.

4 Bugly croaked at Mugly.

5 Pointy tidied up carefully.

Page 43

1 "Will you play with me?" **asked** Miss Snufflebeam.

2 "We are too tired to tidy up," **complained** Mugly and Bugly.

3 "Look at that funny cloud!" **giggled** Miss Snufflebeam.

4 "Maybe you need more magic dust," **suggested** Wizard Whimstaff.

5 "My spell is finished!" **announced** Pointy proudly.

Page 45

Ticked sentences should be:

1 You can start a story by writing about a character.

3 You should plan how you will start and finish, before you start to write.

5 The ending has to follow on from the rest of the story.

Page 47

Circled answers should be:
2 a title
3 bullet points
5 sub-headings

Page 49

1 Find their favourite food bowls.

2 Put equal portions of worm slop into the bowls.

3 Put the bowls down, making sure that you give each frog the right bowl.

4 Stand back while they eat, so that you do not get splashed.

5 Wash the bowls, floor and walls when they have finished.

Page 51

Dark Cave
Precipice
Spelltown
SP11 0FP
4

15th June
1

Dear Pointy,
2
Thanks for your letter. **5** I would love to live with two handsome princes instead of Mugly and Bugly!

See you soon,

Miss Snufflebeam **3**

Pages 52–53

Wizard's Challenge

1 **a** The old lady <u>hobbled</u> across the road.
  b The teacher <u>wrote</u> neatly on the board.
  c The shopkeeper <u>tidied</u> up the shelves.

2 **a** "Well done!" congratulated Wizard Whimstaff.
  b "Where is Pointy?" asked Miss Snufflebeam.
  c "Look at this pretty flower!" exclaimed Miss Snufflebeam.

3 Suggestions are:
  Starting a story: a
  Finishing a story: b and c

4 **a** bullet points — help you to list facts clearly
  b title — says what the piece of writing is about
  c sub-heading — breaks the topic up into smaller sections
  d introduction — says more about what the piece of writing is about
  e ending — your chance to give your view

5 **a** Heat <u>1 litre</u> of water.
  b Add <u>100g</u> of sugar and the juice of three lemons.
  c Simmer for <u>five minutes</u>.

6 True sentences are a and b.
  False sentences are c and d.

Pages 54–61

Test Practice

Spelling

Here is the completed spelling text.

Daisy was excited because she was **going** to the zoo. As she queued **outside** with Mum she could hear monkeys chattering inside, and over the top of the **gate** she could see an elephant's trunk **swaying** in the air.

Inside, the **zoo** was full of people looking at all the animals. Daisy watched the penguins **being** fed. She turned to speak to Mum, but Mum was not there!

Daisy looked and **looked** but she could not **find** Mum. Then she saw something strange. A monkey in a **cage** was waving at her and pointing at something. Daisy looked again and **saw** that the monkey was pointing at Mum!

Building vocabulary

1 bright

2 ugly

3 cool, chilly

4 Many answers are possible, including warm.

Reading

1 Saturday

2 because she did not want to be late for her ballet class

3 that she is not very elegant

4 because the way she moves her arms and legs looks like a frog

5 **Kirstie:** "Saturday! Fantastic!"
  "Look at me, I'm filthy!"

  Meghan: "Never mind that."
  "We have to get to ballet."

6 down Squire Street

7 Mrs Simms

8 raining, drizzle

9 because she was daydreaming about being in the ballet

10 Cinderella

Writing

1 Many answers are possible, but strong endings will provide a definite conclusion to the story, and follow on in a plausible way from events in the beginning and middle sections of the story.

2 Stories will vary, but strong stories will have an opening that grips the attention of the reader. The events in the story should be linked together in a cohesive way, building up towards the ending, which should show how the main dilemma has been resolved. The language throughout should be chosen to support the effects the writer is trying to create.

3 Letters will vary, but the layout should follow the format for informal letters to friends described on page 51.

Glossary

adjective   a word or words used to describe a noun

antonym   a word with a meaning opposite to another, e.g. hot, cold

capital letter   upper case letters used at the start of words that begin sentences and for the names of people, places, days of the week and months of the year, e.g. **K**ate, **S**cotland

comma (,)   shows when to pause, separates clauses, or separates items in a list

compound word   a word made by joining two words together

consonant   any letter of the alphabet except the vowels, **a**, **e**, **i**, **o** and **u**

exclamation mark (!)   can be used instead of a full stop to indicate surprise or that an order has been made, e.g. Hey**!** Stop that**!**

fiction   stories with imaginary characters, settings or events

full stop (.)   signals the end of a sentence

non-fiction   writing that is not fiction, including information texts about real people and places, letters, instructions and reports

noun   a word that names a thing or feeling

past tense   describes things which have happened

plural   more than one of something. Usually made by adding **s**, **es** or **ies**, e.g. car**s**, bush**es**, babies. There are some exceptions, e.g. people, children

prefix   a group of letters added to the beginning of a word to change its meaning, e.g. **un**happy, **dis**obedient

present tense   describes things which are happening now

question mark (?)   can be used in place of a full stop to show that a question has been asked

root word   a word that you can add a prefix or suffix to

sentence   a unit of text that makes sense on its own

singular   one of something, e.g. a dog, the girl

speech marks   surround direct speech. Other punctuation goes inside them, e.g. **"**Hello!**"** said Ian.

suffix   a group of letters added to the end of a root word to change its meaning, e.g. help**less**, bold**ly**

synonym   a word with the same or similar meaning to another, e.g. cold, chilly

tense   tells us when something is happening

verb   a doing or being word

vowel   **a**, **e**, **i**, **o** or **u**. The other letters in the alphabet are consonants